If I Were President

Written by Elaine Hills | Illustrated by Eve Funnell

Published by Orange Hat Publishing 2019

ISBN 978-1-64538-055-9
Library of Congress Control Number: 2019908393

Copyrighted © 2019 by Elaine Hills
All Rights Reserved
If I Were President
Written by Elaine Hills
Illustrated by Eve Funnell

www.orangehatpublishing.com

To Joseph, Nathan,
Tess & Jeanie – with love.
- E.H.

For my mom and siblings: Sonja,
Dawn, Max, Trin and Lara.
- E.F.

If I were president I would have the most *POWERFUL* job in the country!

I would be a *NATURAL LEADER*

overcome *DIFFICULT CHALLENGES*

boost *NATIONAL PRIDE*

and positively affect the course of *AMERICAN AND WORLD HISTORY*

Even now, our past presidents have left lasting impressions on Americans.

They came from many different backgrounds, possessed many different qualities, and yet they all found a way to make America a better place.

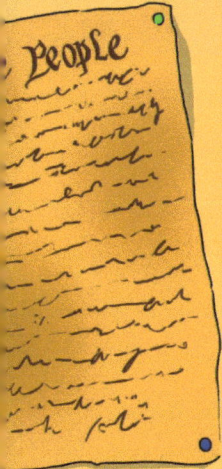

Every president had an occupation before they were elected to the White House.

If I were president, there is a high probability that I would be a lawyer.

Twenty-five past presidents were lawyers!

I might be a teacher like five of our previous presidents.

It is very unlikely that I would be an actor even though our 40th president, Ronald Reagan, was the only actor to serve in our nation's highest office.

HOPE

President Reagan served two consecutive terms from January 1981 to January 1989. He often spoke of Abraham Lincoln's description of the United States as "the last best hope of Earth." In fact, President Reagan's dream came true because by the time he left office, the country was prosperous.

If I were president, I would be at least 35 years of age, and I might be the first woman elected to this office.

I would hope to have the dynamic qualities of all great presidents: HONESTY, BRAVERY, CONFIDENCE, COMMITMENT, and LEADERSHIP, just to name a few.

I trust that I would be able to identify the needs of my country and pursue solutions to those needs.

As president, I would be able to multitask, focus on more than one issue, and the final decision would be mine.

As President Harry S. Truman, our 33rd president, once told a visiting British diplomat,

"I am here to make decisions, and whether they prove right or wrong, I am going to make them."

If I were president, the kind of house
where I grew up would not matter.

Some presidents, such as George Washington, John F. Kennedy, and Franklin Delano Roosevelt all came from wealthy families.

Harry S. Truman, Abraham Lincoln, and Calvin Coolidge grew up on farms with no electricity or running water and had very little money.

However, once these men moved into the White House,

they shared a common feeling of responsibility.

If I were president, I would be a caring president like our 16th president, Abraham Lincoln.

In 1864 he wrote a letter to a woman named Mrs. Bixby, who had lost five of her sons in the Civil War. Presidents George W. Bush and Barack Obama were also known to have contacted parents of lost soldiers to express their condolences.

But it was Jimmy Carter, our 39th president, who stated, "If the misery of others leaves you indifferent and with no feeling of sorrow, then you cannot be called a human being."

President Carter has become well-known the world over as a great example of a caring, compassionate American statesman.

I dream to be like him, as compassion is a priceless gift no matter who you are, president or otherwise.

If I were president, I might have first been a vice president.

If the president in office died, by natural causes or assassination, then I would place my left hand on the Bible, raise my right hand and take the oath of office.

Lyndon Baines Johnson became our 36th president and did just that aboard Air Force One after President John F. Kennedy was assassinated in Dallas, Texas in 1963.

Theodore Roosevelt became our 26th president after the death of President William McKinley in 1901. Roosevelt admitted, "It is a dreadful thing to come into the presidency this way; but it would be a far worse thing to be morbid about it."

Known as Teddy or TR, he not only served two terms, but also inspired the famous Teddy Bear toy, which is beloved around the world to this day.

If I were president, I may have to promise to cut taxes, reduce government spending, and create jobs, like most presidents that have served before me have promised.

I believe that our government, like the hard-working Americans it serves, should live within its means.

Lyndon Baines Johnson, our 36th Commander in Chief, said, "A president's hardest task is not to do what is right, but to know what is right."

Perhaps by the time I am president, the world will already know peace, harmony, prosperity, and unconditional love based on the example set by our country. If not, it is my dream to create this most hoped-for reality.

As I stand before the nation, having taken the solemn oath of office, I will, with God's help, encourage a world filled with KINDNESS, JOY, HARMONY, and PEACE on Earth.

www.ingramcontent.com/pod-product-compliance
Lightning Source LLC
Chambersburg PA
CBHW040713150426

42813CB00062B/2987